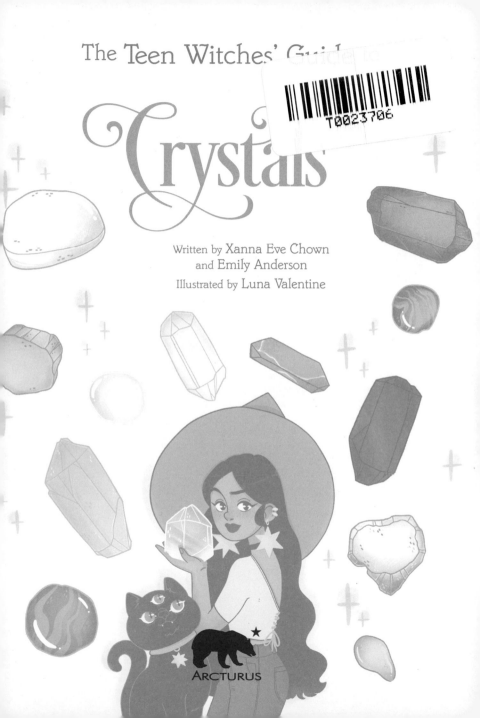

The Teen Witches' Guide to

Crystals

Written by Xanna Eve Chown
and Emily Anderson

Illustrated by Luna Valentine

ARCTURUS

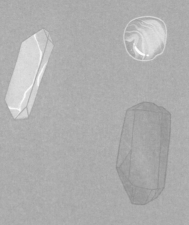

This edition published in 2023 by Arcturus Publishing Limited,
26/27 Bickels Yard, 151–153 Bermondsey Street,
London SE1 3HA

Writers: Xanna Eve Chown and Emily Anderson
Illustrator: Luna Valentine
Designer: Rosie Bellwood
Editor: Donna Gregory

ISBN: 978-1-3988-1518-6
CH010259NT
Supplier 29, Date 0123, PI 00002505
Printed in China

Contents

Note:

The ideas and suggestions in this book are not intended to
be a substitute for conventional medical help. Always consult
your doctor before undertaking any alternative therapy to
ensure that there are no contraindications for your health.

Introduction

You can use crystals to create genuine magic in your life—all you need to do is hold a sparkly geode of amethyst or a smooth, perfect pebble of jade to understand why. As well as seeing its beauty, you will sense its energy. This book will show you how crystals can energize you, heal you, open up your inner wisdom … and more!

When you read about crystals, you will find that you are attracted to certain rocks. These are the ones for you! If you pick up a crystal and find that you can't put it down, it's a sign that it fits perfectly with your needs at this time.

You can use crystals to:

- Boost the energy of a room
- Calm your mind
- Help you sleep
- Divine the future
- Connect to your spiritual side
- Heal your body
- Attract love
- Heighten your psychic ability

Choosing Crystals

A crystal of any size or shape, rough or smooth, has healing properties. It's not about how big or expensive the crystal is—it's about how you work with it. The important thing is your intention, which should be clear and positive to magnify the crystal's benefits. (See page 11 to learn how to charge a crystal with your intention.)

Working with smaller gemstones is far more practical when you want to lay them on your body or carry them in your pocket. You can easily buy small gems called tumblestones, which have been polished into perfectly smooth shapes.

SAY NO TO FAKES!

Try to make sure that the crystals you buy are genuine and natural. The best way to avoid imitations is to buy from crystal stores. Ask the owner where the crystal is from, and have a really good, close look at it. Check its appearance and, most importantly, how it feels to you.

Natural gems

- Gems develop naturally deep in the earth, in rivers, or cliffs, over a long period of time.
- Crystals found in nature often have flaws and are an uneven hue.
- They change over time, fading and becoming cloudy or veined over years of use.

Dyed gems

- Stones such as agate, howlite, jasper, quartz, and granite are often dyed to make them look prettier.
- Most rubies and sapphires have been treated in some way to improve their looks.
- Emeralds often have fractures filled and clarity improved.
- This doesn't take away anything from their quality.

Synthetic gems

- Some crystals are created in laboratories, which makes them more vibrant or uniform in the shade.
- They are not strictly fakes because they contain the same chemical properties as raw gems.
- They won't hold quite the same quality of energy as natural crystals formed over centuries.

Fake crystals

- Fakes can be made from plastic, resin, ceramic, or even painted rocks, designed to look the same as real crystals.
- If there are bubbles in the gem, it's likely to be glass.

Before You Start

CLEANSING YOUR CRYSTALS

Crystals pick up energy from their surroundings and anyone who's handled them. So, before you use them, you need to get rid of any negative or unwanted energy. There are many different ways to cleanse a crystal, and some are specific to each crystal.

Crystal care!

Always check that your crystal won't be damaged before you start! Some can disintegrate in water or fade in too much sunlight.

Five ways to clean a crystal:

- Hold it under clear, running water for a few minutes.
- Leave it outside on the night of a full moon, so it soaks up a full night of moonlight.
- Put it in a pot of herbs, such as rosemary, sage, or lavender, for a few hours.
- Smudging is an ancient way of cleansing energy with a bundle of dried sage. Light the tip, blow out the flame, then pass the crystal through the fragrant smoke.
- Spray it with a couple of drops of crystal cleansing spray. (You can buy this from crystal stores.)

CHARGING YOUR CRYSTALS

Now that your crystals are cleansed, they are ready to be charged with your intention. Your intention is your aim—what you want the crystals to help you with. This could be something specific, such as helping you pass a test, or more general, such as health, wealth, or happiness!

How to set your intention:

- Hold the crystal and state your intention.
- Add the words "this or something better." (You may be pleasantly surprised!)
- Ask your crystal to always work for the highest good for all.
- Finish by thanking the crystal for its help. If you like, you can also ask that it keeps on acting for you, while you continue with your day.

CRYSTALS AND CHAKRAS

Chakras are energy points that run up and down the body. When their energy is balanced, it strengthens your whole system.

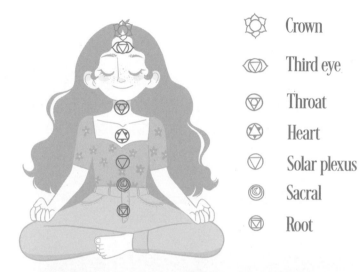

Crown

Third eye

Throat

Heart

Solar plexus

Sacral

Root

How to balance your chakras:

- Lie on your back in a comfortable place.
- Place one crystal on each chakra. Each chakra has several crystals that work best with it. (See page 13.) Choose whichever one you feel most attracted to.
- Let your breathing and body relax, and the crystals will do the rest!

THE SEVEN MAIN CHAKRAS

Crown chakra—Spirituality
Location: Top of head
Gems: Amethyst, clear quartz, selenite

Third eye chakra—Inner wisdom
Location: Between the eyebrows
Gems: Amethyst, black obsidian, blue calcite

Throat chakra—Communication
Location: Middle of neck
Gems: Blue calcite, blue topaz, lapis lazuli,
aquamarine, turquoise

Heart chakra—Love
Location: Middle of chest
Gems: Rose quartz, jade, moldavite

Solar plexus chakra—Confidence
Location: 6 cm (2 in.) above belly button
Gems: Calcite, topaz, citrine

Sacral chakra—Pleasure
Location: 6 cm (2 in.) below belly button
Gems: Citrine, carnelian, moonstone

Root chakra—Grounding
Location: Base of spine
Gems: Tiger's eye, black tourmaline, hematite

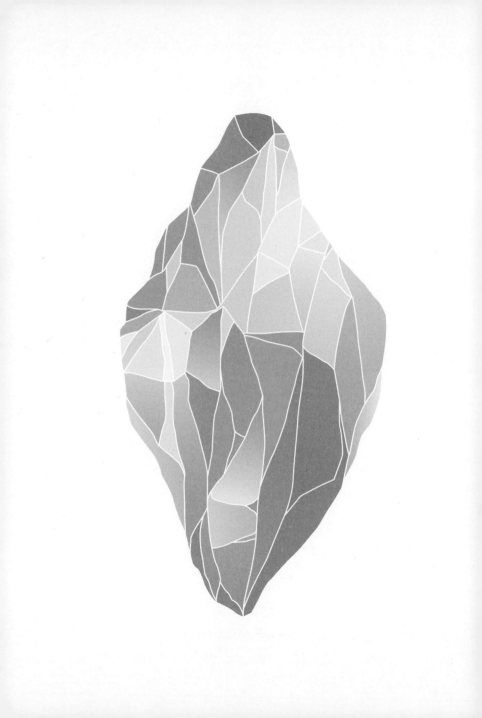

The Best Crystals for Meditation

MEDITATING WITH CRYSTALS

Meditation can bring peace and relaxation to your life. Meditating with crystals can do even more!

- You might connect with higher beings who will help you on your path.
- Your dreams will probably become more vivid, with clear messages or symbolism in them.
- Your ability to sense what's about to happen, or what someone is going to say or do, may get stronger.
- Your connection with others, your creativity, and your destiny will become better than it has ever been.

Have a notebook nearby when you meditate. You may have sudden realizations that you need to write down afterward!

How to meditate with crystals:

- Find somewhere quiet where you can be undisturbed.
- Make yourself comfortable—lie down on the floor, or sit on a cushion or chair.
- Hold your chosen crystals in your hands. Feel their energy flow through your body and the space around you.
- Charge the crystals with an intention for this meditation. (See page 11.)
- Picture those intentions charging up your crystals to help you.
- Continue holding the crystals in your hands, or place them on the chakras they strengthen.
- Close your eyes and relax. Begin by focusing on your breathing. Allow yourself to take some deep breaths in, and some slow breaths out. Inhale. Exhale.
- Allow the energy of the crystal to have an effect—but don't force it or worry if it doesn't. Just continue relaxing and breathing deeply, and see what unfolds. You may get a strong sense to do something new in your life, you might hear messages from other beings, you could even have visions of past life experiences. Just witness it all, knowing that you are safe.
- When you feel like you've come to the end of your meditation, count down from ten to one to bring your awareness back into the room.

AMETHYST

Amethyst is a pale lavender to deep purple quartz, sometimes opaque, sometimes transparent, with white or clear streaks.

BEST FOR

- Developing spirituality
- Deepening meditation
- Boosting creativity

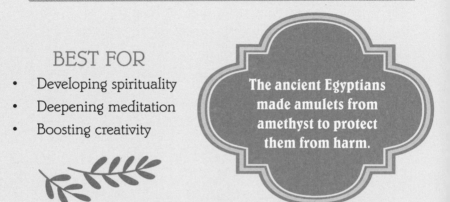

The ancient Egyptians made amulets from amethyst to protect them from harm.

WORKING WITH AMETHYST

Expand your mind

Lie on your back with an amethyst tumblestone placed in the middle of your forehead (third eye chakra). Amethyst boosts this chakra, which increases your psychic abilities.

Feel protected

Hold a large chunk of amethyst in your left hand, resting on your right hand. Sit comfortably and allow your breath to slow and deepen. Imagine the purple energy forming a protective light around your body.

Soothe your sleep

Is it hard for you to fall asleep at night? Place amethyst under your pillow before you go to bed. To ward off nightmares, rub a point of amethyst anticlockwise in the middle of your forehead.

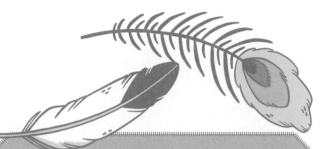

Three ways to beat stress:

- Create a meditation altar in your room with an amethyst geode in the middle. Your altar could be on a table or just a piece of cloth spread on the floor. Whenever you feel stressed, sit next to it and feel the amethyst's powerful calming effects.
- Carry a small piece around in your pocket to protect you from other people's negative energy.
- Hold a single amethyst in your left hand with the point toward your left arm. This will draw calming energy into your body.

ANGELITE

Angelite is white on the outside and light blue inside. Tumbled stones are usually pale blue. It is a highly evolved celestite that has been compressed for millions of years to form nodules.

Crystal care!

Make sure that you keep your angelite dry. It's delicate and can be damaged by water.

BEST FOR

- Communing with higher beings
- Developing psychic powers
- Encouraging clear communication

Angelite is said to vibrate at the frequency of kindness.

WORKING WITH ANGELITE

Help others

Keep a small piece of angelite beside you if you do any readings for others—for instance, when using Tarot cards, astrology, palm reading, or angel cards. This will help you share messages with kindness and clarity.

Make yourself heard

Wear angelite on a choker-style necklace to clear negativity from your throat chakra. This will soften your speech and prevent arguments, or it may help you find the right words if you are nervous about something you have to say.

Remember your dreams

Place a piece of angelite beside your bed if you want to remember the wisdom revealed in your dreams. This gem can help you interpret the dream's symbols when you wake up.

Meditation ritual to receive spiritual guidance:

- **Hold a piece of angelite when you sit in meditation.**
- **Let your gaze rest upon it, eyes half open.**
- **Tune into the higher realms, becoming aware of any guidance you are being sent. This could be messages, symbols, or general sensations.**
- **Take several deep breaths to ground yourself, then thank the crystal.**
- **Write down any messages or feelings in a notebook.**

AZURITE

Azurite is bright to deep blue and indigo, sometimes with light streaks. Its name comes from its beautiful azure-blue appearance, which evolved over the millennia through chemical reactions between copper, hydrogen, carbonate, and oxygen.

BEST FOR

- Connecting with the higher realms
- Reaching the quiet stillness at the heart of meditation
- Receiving healing and psychic experiences

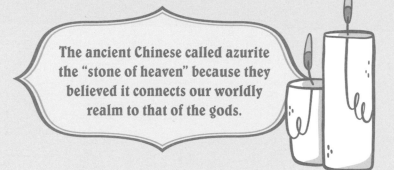

The ancient Chinese called azurite the "stone of heaven" because they believed it connects our worldly realm to that of the gods.

WORKING WITH AZURITE

Open your mind

The energies in this crystal are better released through touching, so hold a smoothed crystal of azurite in your hands during meditation, and ask for it to help open your mind to higher realms.

Beat stress

Wear a pendant of azurite, or carry it in your pocket all day, making sure to smooth your fingers over it often to help clear your mind of stress and tension.

Clear your throat

Wear a piece of azurite as a choker, or place it on the throat area when lying down in meditation. This crystal clears the throat chakra, so that any new ideas and experiences you have received can be perfectly communicated.

Three ways to boost your brain power:

- Place an azurite crystal on your desk to touch during the day and feel its mind-expanding energies.
- Keep a small piece of azurite in your pocket when studying for a test.
- Rub an azurite tumblestone between your fingers to focus your mind while you work.

Black Tourmaline

Black tourmaline, also known as schorl, black or very deep blue, and found in column structures. It often forms in places with high heat and pressure, such as hydrothermal vents and subterranean caverns.

BEST FOR

- Protecting against negative thoughts and energies
- Grounding
- Easing panic attacks and motion sickness

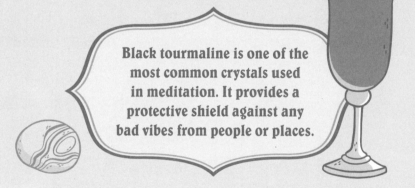

Black tourmaline is one of the most common crystals used in meditation. It provides a protective shield against any bad vibes from people or places.

WORKING WITH BLACK TOURMALINE

Clear your mind

Sit in meditation surrounded with a grid of black tourmaline crystals. This will clear your mind and cleanse your emotions of anything that is weighing you down. (See pages 56–57 for help with making a crystal grid.)

Cleanse your aura

Place a smooth crystal of black tourmaline in your left hand and a piece of selenite crystal in your right hand to cleanse your aura while you meditate.

Get confident

If you are nervous about an upcoming social event, wear a piece of black tourmaline to promote a sense of self-confidence and personal power.

Three ways to banish negativity:

- **Wear a black tourmaline brooch on your left side if you find yourself mixing with angry or draining people.**
- **If you are feeling anxious, depressed, or angry, try sleeping with black tourmaline in your pillowcase.**
- **If there's an area in your home where you feel negativity, place a large piece of black tourmaline here to change the energy.**

BLUE CALCITE

Blue calcite is opaque light blue and white. Calcite takes its name from the Latin and Greek words *calcis* and *khalx*, both meaning "lime."

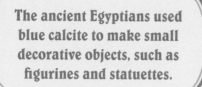

The ancient Egyptians used blue calcite to make small decorative objects, such as figurines and statuettes.

BEST FOR

- Soothing emotions
- Promoting inner peace
- Clear communication

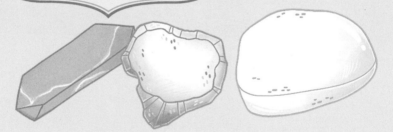

WORKING WITH BLUE CALCITE

Balance your third eye chakra

Place a tumblestone in the middle of your forehead (third eye chakra) while lying down. Balancing this chakra can resolve disagreements and help you to find new ways of looking at situations. Because blue calcite also opens and strengthens the throat chakra, it will help you explain any insights you receive.

Aid your sleep

Sleeping with a chunk of blue calcite on your nightstand can help you drift off into a restful sleep. It also may boost the vividness of your dreams and help you understand their symbolism.

Send healing

Blue calcite is a good crystal for sending healing to people or places that are far away. If you send healing thoughts to a friend or family member while holding a blue calcite crystal, they are sure to reach them.

Meditation ritual to create a more optimistic outlook on life:

- Sit calmly, holding a blue calcite crystal in both hands.
- Say out loud: "I am connecting to a calming universal energy."
- Repeat these words as many times as you like, until you are fully relaxed.
- In this state, your creative side will fill up with ideas and interests.
- Take a few deep breaths to ground yourself, then thank the crystal.
- Be sure to write down all your new ideas!

BLUE TOPAZ

Blue topaz is a light blue, transparent crystal. Topaz is mined in many parts of the world, including China, the United States, Russia, Mexico, and Brazil.

BEST FOR

- Achieving peace
- Revealing truth
- Connecting with higher beings

This gem was revered in ancient Egypt, where it was said to hold mystical powers given by the sun god Ra.

WORKING WITH BLUE TOPAZ

Solve problems

If you need to think through a complicated problem, meditate with blue topaz first. Let its power flow through you for a few minutes, then set your mind to work with renewed energy.

Find yourself

Gazing into the gentle blue of this crystal can help you connect with your true self. It will highlight any patterns in your actions that may be keeping you from fully being your true self.

Set goals

Set goals while sitting quietly with blue topaz. Try and imagine all the details of how these goals will unfold, and the positive effect they will have on your life. Then fill your crystal with that creative, can-do energy, and trust that everything will turn out well.

Meditation ritual to listen to your inner guidance:

- Lie on your back with one small tumblestone on your throat chakra and one on your third eye chakra.
- Think about the situation that you are unclear about.
- The blue topaz will help you understand what you would like or not like in your life.
- Spend a few minutes relaxing as you let these ideas reach you.
- When you are finished, be sure to ground yourself with a few deep breaths.
- Thank the crystals, then write down what you have learned in a notebook.

CLEAR QUARTZ

Clear quartz is a clear crystal that is shimmery in the light. It is the most common, yet most powerful, mineral on Earth.

Crystal care!

Because it's such a strong booster of energies, make sure you cleanse your clear quartz regularly. (See page 10.)

BEST FOR

- Energizing
- Boosting your psychic ability
- Magnifying the powers of other crystals

Clear quartz is known as the "master healer." It was a magical tool for the Celts, Maya, Aztecs, Egyptians, and Native Americans, who believed these crystals to be the divine incarnate.

WORKING WITH CLEAR QUARTZ

Connect with higher realms

Program clear quartz with your intention to connect with higher beings, and it will help with this every time you meditate with it. Keep a note of any feelings or impressions you get while meditating, as these are all communication.

Love yourself

Sit quietly, and hold a quartz crystal on the heart chakra. The crystal will dissolve any blocks to self-acceptance and love.

Soothe your sleep

Sleep next to some clear quartz, and let it help you drift into a deep sleep full of memorable and meaningful dreams.

Meditation ritual to achieve your goals:

- Write down your main goal on a piece of paper.
- Now, imagine that you have achieved this goal. Really think about it in detail—what would happen, how you would feel, and how your life would change for the better.
- Sit with a chunk of clear quartz in your lap and picture this energy charging the crystal.
- When you are finished, wrap the crystal in the paper with your goal written on it, and sleep with it next to your bed.

LABRADORITE

Labradorite is murky green, black, or smoky white with a rainbow shimmer of hues including bright blue, pale green, coppery red, and flashes of gold. Its name comes from Labrador in Canada, where it was discovered.

BEST FOR

- Attracting magic
- Protection
- Boosting courage

The dazzling rainbow inside this crystal is said to look like the aurora borealis—or the northern lights—where the Inuit people believe the crystal came from.

WORKING WITH LABRADORITE

Protect yourself

Labradorite protects anyone who wants to travel to higher realms when they meditate. Keep a small stone nearby to keep you safe on your inner journeys and protect you from negative energy.

Open your chakras

Ask labradorite to open all your chakras. Then hold a crystal, and picture its rainbow shades flooding each of your chakras with powerful light, one by one, from the root chakra to the crown. (See page 13 to locate your chakras.)

Bring balance

Labradorite is known as the "stone of balance." When you meditate with this crystal, it can help you balance the dark and light inside you, letting you shine even brighter.

Meditation ritual to energize:

- Sit outside holding a crystal. Labradorite is strongest at dusk and dawn when the light is changing.
- Feel the rainbow energy moving through you, transforming your body into magical rays shining with blue, green, purple, violet, and gold.
- Open your eyes; notice how calm and energized you feel.
- Thank the crystal, and take a few deep breaths to ground yourself.

SELENITE

Selenite is pure white or translucent. It grows naturally in wands. When activating your selenite, try gently rubbing it.

Crystal care!

Selenite can be cleansed in water that the full moonlight has shone into. Never leave it in water, because it will dissolve.

BEST FOR

- Connecting to the higher realms
- Deflecting negativity
- Encouraging psychic insight

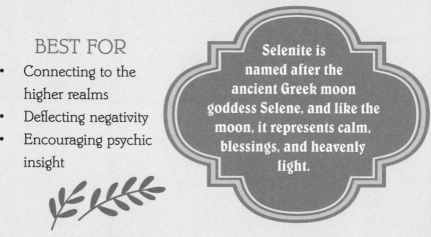

Selenite is named after the ancient Greek moon goddess Selene, and like the moon, it represents calm, blessings, and heavenly light.

WORKING WITH SELENITE

Connect with higher beings

Lie on your back with a selenite wand on your heart chakra pointing toward your head, and place another on the floor with the point just touching your crown chakra. (See page 13 for the positions of the chakras.) Breathe deeply and feel the calm this crystal brings. You may receive guidance about the past or future, which could take the form of symbols in your mind.

Create an energy grid

You can create energy grids at home using several of these wands. Lie down in the middle of a selenite grid and nothing negative will come to you. (See pages 56–57 for help with making a crystal grid.)

Meditation ritual to bring peace:

- Sit upright. Breathe in deeply, and imagine pure white light filling your body. Breathe out and relax.
- Hold your selenite in your left hand. Place your right hand underneath the left, cradling your crystal in your lap.
- Look gently at your selenite and feel yourself glowing with its white energy.
- Hold the crystal to the top of your head (crown chakra), and let the white light of the selenite enter it.
- Move the gem to your forehead (third eye chakra), and hold it there for a few minutes.
- Know that you are safe, and let your mind travel where it wants to go—maybe to familiar places or even to the stars!
- Don't forget to take a few deep breaths to ground yourself, and thank the crystal when you are finished.

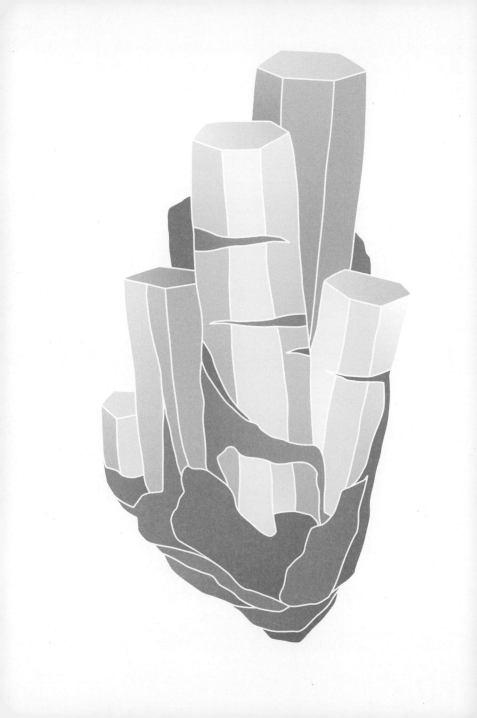

The Best Crystals for Manifestation

Manifesting Your Desires

Manifestation means turning thoughts into reality. Everything that we want starts off as a thought—whether it's to be more successful at school, kick-start a healthy habit, or even get your crush to notice you! You can use crystals to help you manifest these thoughts, making your dreams come true. Here's how:

Find out what's blocking you

Meditate with the right crystal to discover what's keeping you from reaching your full potential. It could be fear, pain, sadness, or exhaustion. Take time to be kind to yourself, and know that these feelings will pass in time.

Have a gratitude attitude

Remember to be grateful for all you have. There is always something you can focus on in the present to be thankful for. Feeling gratitude increases the flow of positive energy around you, bringing more wonderful things your way.

Meditate on what you really want

Meditating with crystals will open up your chakras to boost your energy and attract the opportunities that you need to succeed.

Set an intention

Try setting an intention with a positive affirmation. Picture your life working out the way you want it to, and send that visualization into the crystal to charge it with your intention.

Empower yourself

Keep the charged crystal in your pocket, or sleep with it under your pillow. You could also wear it as a necklace to stay in contact with its powerful energy all day. This will empower you to make the right decisions, which will lead you to the right path.

CITRINE

Citrine is a pale yellow to amber and orange quartz. The yellow comes from impurities in iron that were present when this type of quartz was formed. Its name comes from the Latin word *citrina*, meaning yellow.

Crystal care!

Citrine never needs to be cleansed, but to boost its radiance, leave citrine in sunlight from dawn until noon on the summer solstice. Just don't leave it in the sun too long or it may crack.

BEST FOR

- Strengthening inner wisdom
- Boosting creativity
- Manifesting wealth

Long ago, merchants placed this crystal in their vaults as a magic charm to keep their money safe.

Ignite your imagination

Gaze into a piece of citrine, and imagine the clear energy of the morning sunlight surrounding your body. Meditating with citrine helps activate your imagination … This is useful because you need to imagine the future you want before you can bring it into being!

Wise spending

Citrine is said to encourage wise spending decisions. Take a tumblestone with you when you go shopping to make sure you don't buy anything you will later regret, or keep a small piece in your wallet to protect your bank card!

Citrine ritual to attract money:

- This is an early morning ritual, so make sure that you do it at the beginning of the day.
- Burn a yellow candle next to a piece of citrine to charge the crystal.
- Picture (and really feel) your desire becoming reality while holding the crystal in your dominant hand. (This is your right hand, if you are right-handed, your left if you are left-handed!)
- Imagine this vision charging the crystal with the energy needed to help you put plans into action.
- Keep the fully charged crystal in your wallet to attract wealth.

Green Aventurine

Green aventurine is a light to mid green, opaque, oxide quartz often containing bright inclusions of mica, making it glisten when polished. It is usually green but also forms in blue, red, reddish brown, orange, peach, yellow, silver, or dusty purple.

Crystal care!

You should cleanse this crystal often as it absorbs negative energy. Place it outside to fully recharge overnight, covered in a handful of soil.

BEST FOR

- Creating opportunities
- Bringing good luck
- Manifesting prosperity

Traditionally in central Asia, people believed that green aventurine improved eyesight, so sculptors would decorate statues with it to show their subject's "visionary" power.

WORKING WITH GREEN AVENTURINE

Boost your luck

Sometimes called the "stone of opportunity," green aventurine is the crystal to have with you if you need good luck! Try wearing it as a necklace, brooch, or earrings, or carry a tumblestone around in your pocket.

Improve your mood

Meditate with a piece of green aventurine when you are angry, stressed, or sad, and it will absorb the negative energy. Picture the negative emotions draining into the crystal, leaving you cleansed. When you are done, cleanse the crystal and leave it to recharge. (See page 42.)

Get happy

Working with green aventurine can give you a renewed zest for life, which can help create better luck. It will show you that the positive energy you put out in the world comes back to you—which is what manifesting good outcomes is all about!

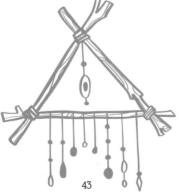

GREEN JADE

Jade is the name given to two different minerals: dark-green, glassy-looking nephrite and lighter, dull and waxy jadeite. The best way to tell them apart is to tap them with a hard object—nephrite will chime a musical note, jadeite won't. But they both help protect your finances and attract more wealth.

Jade is the sacred crystal of the New Zealand Maori, who call it greenstone.

BEST FOR

- Healing the heart to attract love and friendship
- Balancing mind, body, and spirit
- Helping you to act on your dreams

WORKING WITH GREEN JADE

Encourage meaningful dreams

Place a small piece of jade on your forehead for a couple of minutes before going to sleep. This will help you remember and understand the messages in your dreams.

Fill yourself with love

Hold green jade to your heart and you will feel its strong
energies pulsing through your entire body. Picture the
crystal healing your heart and supporting your spirit to
move forward with love. Use this renewed energy to turn
your desires into reality.

Be yourself

Let this crystal remind you that we are all spiritual beings
on a journey, and that we are all doing the best we can.
Wear a green jade pendant every day to help you become
more of who you really are in each and every moment.

Boost your studies

Place some green jade on your desk to boost success in
your work. Jade can keep your mind sharp when you are
dealing with facts and figures.

Keep calm

Rub a small, smooth piece of green jade with your
fingers. This will bring calm if you're dealing with difficult
situations or if you feel overwhelmed by daily events.

PYRITE

Pyrite is a sparkly, silvery gold, found in clusters or cubes. It is lighter, harder, and more brittle than real gold. Its name comes from the Greek word *pyr* or *pyros*, which means fire, because it creates sparks when struck with metal or crystal.

BEST FOR

- Attracting wealth
- Encouraging yourself to build better habits
- Boosting your leadership skills

A common nickname for pyrite is fool's gold. This is because its appearance can fool people into believing that it really is gold!

WORKING WITH PYRITE

Manifest success

Every morning, hold some pyrite in your hand while looking at your reflection in a mirror. Gaze lovingly into your eyes and say, "I am worthy of success now."

Awaken your inner warrior

This crystal is associated with the qualities needed for success: a strong will, focus, and determination. Keep a highly polished tumblestone in your pocket all day, and use it as a mirror to remind yourself that you have all these qualities.

Encourage creativity

Pyrite is an excellent crystal to carry in your schoolbag because it helps you feel connected to long-term projects.

Clear stress

Place a piece of pyrite on your desk to bring its bright, high-frequency energy to the area. This energy will clear any stress caused by working too hard.

ROSE QUARTZ

Rose Quartz has a rose-pink hue from traces of titanium, iron, or manganese. It usually occurs in massive form, though it sometimes grows in clusters of small crystals. It varies in clarity from opaque to translucent to a foggy transparency.

Beads made of rose quartz have been found dating back to 7000 BCE, from the region known as Mesopotamia, now Iraq.

BEST FOR

- Manifesting unconditional love
- Attracting romance
- Encouraging healing

WORKING WITH ROSE QUARTZ

Attract romance

Use rose quartz to set up an altar in the far right section of
your bedroom, as you stand at the door. Your altar can be
a small table, the seat of a chair, or even a piece of cloth
spread on the floor. On a small table, upturned box, or
any other surface covered with pretty fabric, place a chunk
of rose quartz in the middle, along with two red or pink
candles to light while you meditate. Add other symbols of
love, such as a bunch of roses or other blooms, pictures of
happy couples from magazines, or pairs of ornaments.

Meditation ritual to welcome love into your life:

- Lie down on your back in a comfortable place. Take a
  few deep breaths and close your eyes.
- Place a small piece of rose quartz over the middle of your
  chest where your heart chakra sits.
- Breathe in its energy, imagining its soft pink hue filling
  your whole body with love.
- See this gentle pink energy of love filling your heart
  chakra. Let it melt away any negativity.
- Keep breathing in that soothing, warm energy of love
  from the rose quartz as you go about your day.

Tiger's Eye

Tiger's eye is a type of quartz crystal that is harvested mostly in Africa and Australia. The crystals are very beautiful because of the unusual brown and golden silky swirls or stripes that run through the stone.

BEST FOR

- Bringing luck and bravery in new ventures
- Boosting creativity
- Encouraging willpower

Ancient Egyptians believed that tiger's eye transmitted the power of the sun god Ra, and the Romans would carry this gem to battle to encourage bravery.

Stop fights

Tiger's eye can help build better family relations. Place several small crystals around your home to balance and soothe relationships. It is one of the best gems to have around if you are trying to resolve an argument!

Attract money

Keep a small, polished piece of tiger's eye in a pot and add a small coin every day for a year. Keep this pot in a warm place, in the prosperity area of your home (far left corner from the front door) to attract wealth.

Three ways to use tiger's eye to help you study:

- Tiger's eye is a great crystal with which to meditate if you are starting a new project. It will guide you to make balanced decisions that will bring success.
- Keep a piece of this crystal on your desk, at home or at school, to manifest good fortune.
- A tumblestone in your pocket will help you stay focused and use your talents wisely.

Titanium Rainbow Quartz

Titanium rainbow quartz is a man-made gem that has been specially bonded with titanium to give it a rainbow shimmer.

This crystal is often called "the manifestation crystal." It is the most powerful of the coated quartz crystals because titanium (the metal of power) boosts the effects of quartz.

BEST FOR

- Energizing all your chakras
- Awakening your true self
- Finding creative ways to express yourself

WORKING WITH TITANIUM RAINBOW QUARTZ

Be yourself

Wear titanium rainbow quartz, or carry a small piece in your pocket, to manifest more energy and enjoyment in your life. This crystal is said to awaken parts of you that have been sleeping, meaning that you can reveal more of your true self to the world.

Get writing

This is a great crystal to boost your creativity and help you express yourself in words. Place a cluster of titanium rainbow quartz on your desk to inspire your writing—whether it's texts, emails, or even a book that you are writing!

Five minute rainbow meditation:

- Spend five minutes a day gazing at the rainbow hues of this crystal.
- Ask it to clear your aura of any blocks that may be holding you back from your goals.
- Picture the crystal connecting you with the guidance that you need. It will help you get in touch with the higher realms when you need inspiration or wisdom. This will give you the confidence to ask the universe for what you truly desire.

CRYSTAL RECIPES

Combining different crystals can create powerful recipes to attract love, wealth, and success into your life.

TO ATTRACT MONEY INTO YOUR LIFE

1. Locate the wealth corner of your bedroom. This is the back left corner, when standing at the doorway, facing in.
2. Make sure that this area is completely clutter-free.
3. Place a piece of green jade, tiger's eye, and pyrite in a small bowl in this area.

TO ATTRACT LOVE INTO YOUR LIFE

1. Find a piece of amethyst and rose quartz that are of similar sizes.
2. Place them on a piece of paper and draw a heart around them.
3. Cut out the heart, and put it on your nightstand with the amethyst and rose quartz in the middle.

TO MANIFEST SUCCESS

1. Place citrine, green aventurine, and black tourmaline on your desk while you study.

2. When you are finished studying, put the crystals into a pouch.
3. Sleep with the pouch under your pillow or on your nightstand.

TO ACCESS INNER WISDOM

1. Hold a piece of moonstone in one hand and a piece of rose quartz in the other.
2. Concentrate on the question that you want your inner wisdom to answer.
3. Close your eyes and picture the crystals' energy flowing through you, until you are positively glowing with divine charm.
4. Now open your eyes. Your inner wisdom will be awake, you will be aware of your deeper emotions, and you will know the truth.

CREATE A CRYSTAL GRID

Combining a few crystals in a grid makes them even more powerful. Their energies will be mixed with the sacred geometry of the formation you lay them out in, and this boosts their ability to attract what you desire.

THE SEED OF LIFE

You will need:
Paper and pen
Clear quartz
Iolite
Pyrite
Citrine
Green Jade

Create the grid

- Draw the Seed of Life pattern shown opposite. Its symbol combined with the crystals will help you succeed at your goal.

- Make sure the crystals you use have been cleansed and charged with energy. (See pages 10–11.)

- On the first day of the new moon, put the clear quartz in the middle to boost the other crystals' energies. Then place the other gems, in positions that feel right to you.

- As you're adding each crystal to the grid, really take the time to feel its frequency and embed it with your intention—to manifest love, wealth, or success.

- Meditate on the crystals, asking them to work to manifest your desires at the right time.

- Leave the grid untouched for a month, so that it has time to work its magic.

The Seed of Life geometry pattern is a sacred design, made up of seven circles that represent infinite possible paths.

The Best Crystals for Your Home

CRYSTALS IN YOUR HOUSE

Having crystals in your home can only make you happier! Choose the right crystals for each area of your living space and they can protect, bring peace, or energize. Make sure that the crystals are cleansed and programmed with your intention before you use them. (See pages 10–11 to discover how to do this.)

DO TRY THIS AT HOME!

- Certain crystals dotted around your bedroom will emit their energy into the areas they are positioned in. Celestite and blue calcite can lift your spirits, while amethyst and clear quartz can help you connect to higher realms when you meditate.

- A small bowl of crystals will keep the atmosphere in that room balanced and upbeat, even if there's been a drama. Blue lace agate is said to be calming, while a large piece of selenite can generate a peaceful, positive atmosphere.

- Simple crystal tricks include keeping a piece of citrine in your wallet for increased wealth, or putting a piece of moss agate under your anxious pet's bed to help it settle down.

- Crystals can help our health by protecting us from the effects of the electromagnetic frequency and radiation from modern technology. Placing black tourmaline or smoky quartz between you and your device can soak up any potentially damaging energy.

AMBER

Amber is mostly transparent golden, but it can sometimes be yellow, brown, blue, violet, green, or black. Amber is not actually a crystal—it is fossilized resin from ancient coniferous trees.

BEST FOR

- Happiness in the home
- Attracting love
- Keeping calm

Because it sometimes contains fossilized plants or insects, amber was said to contain the essence of life and was seen as sacred by many ancient peoples.

WORKING WITH AMBER

Find love

If it's new love you'd like in your life, charge a piece of amber with this intention and wear it as a pendant! It will connect with the solar plexus chakra and sacral chakra to give you the energy to act on your desires.

Stop headaches

Amber encourages the body to heal itself and was even used as a protective amulet in ancient Egypt. Sit next to a small piece of amber while studying to keep a clear head and prevent any stress headaches.

Three ways to transform negative energy:

- **Wear an amber necklace to absorb negative energy or transform it into positive energy.**
- **A large piece of amber in the middle of your bedroom can get help banish feelings of sadness and anxiety.**
- **Create a comfortable, cushioned area in your bedroom where you can sit and look at a piece of glowing amber every day in winter to chase away any cold-weather blues.**

BLACK OBSIDIAN

Black obsidian is pure, glossy black or very dark brown. Obsidian is made of earth, water, and fire and formed from molten lava in the latter stages of volcanic eruptions.

Crystal care!

Do not put obsidian on the floor or anywhere it might get neglected—it needs to be regularly cleansed of all the negative energy it absorbs. Do this by placing it under any light source.

BEST FOR

- Protection
- Getting rid of negative vibes
- Soaking up stress

Black obsidian was once polished and used for mirrors by the Maya and other ancient civilizations.

WORKING WITH BLACK OBSIDIAN

Clear negative energy

Having obsidian in your home makes it a truly safe haven. It is known as a "psychic vacuum cleaner," because it clears negative energy from its environment. It will put up a barrier to protect you from unwanted guests or bullies, and allow you to retreat from the world for a short while.

Boost your strength

Black obsidian is said to deepen your connection with nature. Place a large piece on a table or wall in your yard or garden, and you will feel more in tune with the physical world.

Energize your studies

If you are finding your schoolwork hard, place obsidian in the area of your home connected to career. (This is the left-hand corner as you face inward from the front door.) A small sphere, or a bowl of tumbled obsidian crystals, will help rebalance your energy, soak up stress,  and inspire creativity … so that your life can flow smoothly again!

BLUE LACE AGATE

Blue lace agate is very pale blue with white or darker blue lines. A pretty crystal, with delicate bands and patterns that look like lace, it is a type of chalcedony, a mineral in the quartz family.

BEST FOR

- Creating a calm atmosphere
- Promoting clear communication
- Helping healers

Blue lace agate is cool to the touch, and is said to help keep insect bites from itching when held against them.

WORKING WITH BLUE LACE AGATE

Soothe your sleep

Placed on a bedside table, the soothing, tranquil energy of blue lace agate will greatly relieve anxiety, stress, or nervousness.

Build self-confidence

Blue lace agate helps you find your voice. It builds self-confidence and lets you speak your truth with kindness. Wear it around your neck, so that it really works its magic on your throat chakra.

Stop arguments

If you find that you keep getting into family arguments that make you stressed and angry, light a blue candle surrounded by pieces of blue lace agate to bring calm back into your home.

Use a compass to find out which direction your house is facing, then place a small piece of blue lace agate in the following places to achieve health, wealth, and happiness:

North—for your life to flow more smoothly
East—for improved health
Southeast—for increased wealth
Southwest—to boost romance

CELESTINE

Celestite is usually clusters and geodes of light blue, but it can be found in white, orange, red, and brown. Its name comes from a Greek word meaning "heavenly."

BEST FOR

- Connecting to the higher realms
- Creating a calming atmosphere
- Soothing relationships

The world's largest-known geode is made of celestite. It was found on an island on Lake Erie, in North America. The owner of the land converted it into a crystal cave for visitors.

WORKING WITH CELESTITE

Deepen your meditation

Lie down with pieces of celestite placed on the throat, third eye, and crown chakras (see page 13), and you will float effortlessly into a deep meditation. Fears and insecurities will disappear, as you realize you are safe and protected by higher beings.

Promote peace

If a room in your home feels chaotic, put a piece of this light blue crystal in a prominent place to create peaceful harmony. Celestite has a gentle, uplifting energy that cleanses the surrounding area, allowing you to relax and feel the presence of the higher realms.

Sleep tight

Because of its ability to bring calm, celestite is a perfect crystal for the bedroom to enable you to smoothly drift into sleep. It will help you go on fantastic journeys in your dreams and remember them in the morning, too! A small piece of celestite under your pillow will help soothe any fears brought on by the darkness.

FLUORITE

Fluorite comes in green, blue, purple, clear, and brown, sometimes all at once! It glows when exposed to UV light.

Crystal care!

You should cleanse fluorite often—it is such a protective crystal that it soaks up a lot of negative energy. It likes to be washed in a stream or placed in a bowl of water overnight.

BEST FOR

- Protection
- Organization
- Helping you move forward

Fluorite was used in ancient Rome to make expensive drinking cups.

WORKING WITH FLUORITE

Boost your home's energy

Fluorite helps you organize everything, from the clutter in your bedroom to your relationships! Having fluorite in your home will bring structure to your daily life, help you learn and think quicker, and heighten your spiritual awareness.

Create harmony

A chunk of fluorite will encourage an uplifting atmosphere that makes friends feel relaxed when they visit. It gets rid of negative opinions and creates a sense of harmony. Yellow fluorite is great to have around if you are working on a group project, because it encourages cooperation.

Out and about

Keep this crystal's qualities working when you are not at home by wearing fluorite in earrings or holding and rubbing a smoothed pebble of it as a palm stone.

Three ways to use fluorite to connect with nature:

- Place a chunk of green fluorite in the yard or garden to attract butterflies.
- Meditate outside with any shade of fluorite to help you tune in to nature.
- Use green fluorite to heal damaged plants by charging it with that intention, holding it over the affected area, then placing it in the plant pot.

Jet

Jet is black like coal, but is usually polished. It is not a crystal—it is a fossilized wood from ancient times.

Crystal care!

Bury jet in soil overnight to cleanse it. If you've inherited something made of jet that's been worn for generations, make sure you cleanse it carefully before use, because it will have soaked up so much of the previous wearer's energy.

BEST FOR

- Protection
- Absorbing negativity
- Grounding

If you're attracted to a piece of jet, you are likely to be an old soul, with many memories of past life experiences!

WORKING WITH JET

Bury anxieties

Jet works in the bedroom to reduce anxiety around sleep. If you have many worries, talk about them while holding a lump of jet. Then bury the rock overnight, either in a pot filled with soil or in the yard or garden, to take away your fears.

Increase your wealth

Use jet to balance your finances by placing it in the wealth corner at the far left back corner of your home.

Cleanse other crystals

Jet is a purifier of all other crystals. Simply place your crystals with jet in a bowl and leave overnight.

Three ways to banish bad vibes:

- **Place a piece of jet facing the front or back door to keep negative energy away.**
- **If your home is full of sadness, place jet in the main living area.**
- **Wear a piece of jet to help you come to terms with the loss of a loved one.**

Moss Agate

Moss agate is milky white or translucent with tendrils of manganese or iron that have made patterns that look like moss. Sometimes they can be dark green with blue inclusions.

BEST FOR

- Connecting with nature
- Calming animals
- Encouraging new beginnings

European farmers used to hang moss agate from trees and around the horns of oxen, to encourage successful harvests.

WORKING WITH MOSS AGATE

Perk up your plants

Plant this crystal with your plants in a pot or flowerbed, to ensure that they stay healthy and grow well. Moss agate helps you communicate with higher beings who can help with the success of your plants.

Be positive

Moss agate can bring calm to your home, especially when placed in your living area. It works to improve the positive parts of people's personalities and helps everyone get along better.

Think deep

This is a wonderful crystal to place in your bedroom to help you quietly contemplate your spiritual growth and the interconnectedness of life.

Three ways to attract wealth and success:

- If you're starting a new project, place a small chunk of moss agate on your desk while you work.
- If someone you know wants a promotion or better pay at work, give them a small crystal as a good luck charm.
- Keep a tumblestone in your piggy bank or money box to help attract wealth.

Smoky Quartz

Smoky quartz is a translucent quartz turning yellowish, brown, or black. It was originally called "morion" when it was discovered and used by the ancient Druids.

BEST FOR

- Grounding
- Protection
- Clearing negative energy

Smoky quartz is the national gem of Scotland. It is one of the power crystals on the handle of the Scottish dagger, still part of the country's national outfit today.

WORKING WITH SMOKY QUARTZ

Connect to the earth

Linking with the root chakra, this powerful crystal will increase your connection to the Earth. Stand on the grass with a piece of smoky quartz in your non-dominant hand (this is your left hand if you are right-handed) pointing downward, and feel any negativity drain out of you and into the ground.

See spirits

You may see more psychic phenomena such as ghosts, spirit guides, or UFOs when wearing or carrying smoky quartz because it makes them easier to notice.

Three ways to promote positivity:

- Use smoky quartz in all the areas of your house to put a stop to bad moods or nasty comments that bring you down.
- Keep a chunk of smoky quartz beside your bed, and let its energy lift depression and promote positive thoughts.
- Place a tumblestone under your pillow to keep your mind from racing while you are trying to get to sleep.

TURQUOISE

Turquoise is a copper metal material containing greenish speckles. The turquoise mineral is considered one of the highest-value minerals in the world by most collectors.

BEST FOR

- Boosting leadership qualities
- Clearing communication
- Encouraging prosperity and success

Turquoise is sometimes called "the campaigner's crystal" because it brings strength and leadership to people who want to protect the environment and human rights.

WORKING WITH TURQUOISE

Create calm

At home, turquoise brings creativity and inner calm, along with strength, ambition, and alertness. Place stones around the house to create an atmosphere of well-being, success, and good luck.

Boost romance

Keeping turquoise in your room encourages romance and clear communication between each other.

Promote positivity

As a purification crystal, turquoise clears negativity from the mind. If you're feeling exhausted, panicky, or sad, rest while holding a small tumblestone, and let it lift your low mood.

Conquer shyness

If you have to speak in public, wearing turquoise as a necklace will calm your nerves. It will help you overcome any shyness, too. It works by balancing the throat chakra, which lets you express yourself effectively.

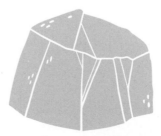

Household Problems

For most household problems, there's a crystal that can help!
Always make sure you cleanse your crystals before use, and charge
them with your intent. (See pages 10–11.)

Messy, chaotic house?
• Fluorite brings harmony and structure, and helps clear the clutter.

Family arguments?
• Blue lace agate on a dining room table makes talking easier.
• Amber in your living room transforms negative vibes into positive.

Noise outside?
• Rose quartz next to the wall closest to the noise promotes peace.

Sleep problems?
• Amazonite or ametrine in your bedroom helps encourage a
  healthier lifestyle.
• Jet in the bedroom soothes you to sleep and repels bad dreams.

Dying houseplants?
• Moss agate in the soil will keep your pot plants from wilting.

KEY CRYSTALS FOR EACH AREA

Front door
• To protect the whole home, choose smoky quartz, black
  tourmaline, or jet to go in the doorway.

Living area
• A large piece of rose quartz or jade will spread love and harmony
  throughout the whole home.

- A wand of selenite on a side table will fill the place with positive light.
- Tiger's eye will help bring harmony to family relationships.

Kitchen or dining room
- Amber on the dining room table encourages healthy eating.
- Citrine in the middle of the room keeps conversation positive while you eat.
- For creative, confident cooking, keep carnelian in the kitchen.

Bedroom
- For deep sleep, place a small, smooth crystal of amethyst or moonstone under your pillow or bed.
- Encourage good dreams by placing a piece of rose quartz on your nightstand.

On your desk
- To combat stress, a black obsidian sphere will help you regain your balance.
- For creativity, place clear quartz nearby, but balance it with lapis lazuli so you don't work too late.
- Celestite will get your creative juices flowing.

Bathroom
- Jade helps restore your tired body while you wash or shower.
- Clear quartz energizes you in the morning while you brush your teeth.
- Turquoise brings inspiration while you soak in the bathtub.

WHICH CRYSTAL FOR WHICH ZODIAC SIGN?

Each zodiac sign has certain crystals that work best with it. Boost your astrological traits by wearing these crystals as a pendant or earrings, carrying a small stone in your pocket, or placing them in your home.

ARIES (MARCH 21–APRIL 20)
Diamond, bloodstone, pyrite, hematite, jasper

TAURUS (APRIL 21–MAY 21)
Rose quartz, emerald, peridot

GEMINI (MAY 22–JUNE 21)
Citrine, white sapphire, ametrine, green aventurine

CANCER (JUNE 22–JULY 22)
Moonstone, pearl, selenite, sodalite

LEO (JULY 23–AUGUST 23)
Carnelian, topaz, tiger's eye, amber, clear quartz

VIRGO (AUGUST 24–SEPTEMBER 22)
Moss agate, blue sapphire, amazonite, yellow aragonite

LIBRA (SEPTEMBER 23–OCTOBER 23)

Lapis lazuli, celestite, rose quartz

SCORPIO (OCTOBER 24–NOVEMBER 22)

Black obsidian, apache tear, coral, labradorite

SAGITTARIUS (NOVEMBER 23–DECEMBER 21)

Turquoise, ruby, azurite, rhodochrosite, iolite

CAPRICORN (DECEMBER 22–JANUARY 20)

Black onyx, garnet, jet, smoky quartz

AQUARIUS (JANUARY 21–FEBRUARY 18)

Amethyst, blue lace agate, angelite

PISCES (FEBRUARY 19–MARCH 20)

Jade, aquamarine, purple fluorite, kyanite

Cusp dates

If you were born a day either side of the dates shown for your zodiac sign, you were born on the "cusp" of two signs. The exact time of the Sun's entry into each zodiac sign varies slightly every year. You can check online to discover the exact moment the Sun moved into each zodiac sign in the year you were born.

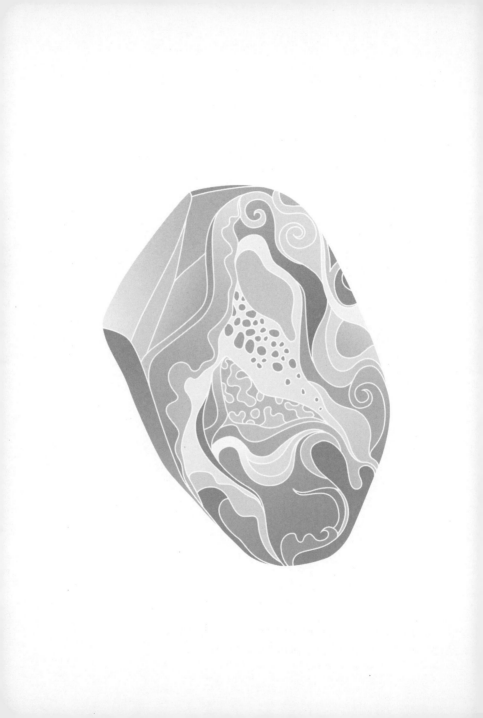

The Best
Crystals for
Healing

Healing with Crystals

Crystals heal by vibrating at a frequency that influences your mind, body, and spirit. You can use your inner wisdom to help you choose the right crystal for your specific healing needs. The energy a crystal gives out depends on what it looks like, what it's made of, and the intention it has been programmed with.

> If you have a specific problem you want help with, such as a bruised knee or a headache, simply place a small crystal on it, or hold it close to the area for as long as you can, imagining its healing energy working its way to the problem.

CLEARING AND ACTIVATING THE CHAKRAS

You can use crystals to cleanse your chakras by placing them on your body. (See page 13.)

- Place the correct ones down the middle of your body while lying down in meditation.
- Relax for 10 minutes to let the crystals' energy have an effect on the chakras beneath them, cleansing, balancing, and energizing your whole system.

RAINBOW MEDITATION

This will really make your aura sparkle. It is a powerful meditation, so there is no need to do it more than once a week.

- Pick crystals that match the shades of the rainbow: red, orange, yellow, green, blue, and purple. Red crystals will energize you, green will nurture you, and orange boosts creativity. Pink will fill you with love, blue helps clear communication, and purple links to higher realms.

- Lay the crystals out on the floor in a circle, and sit inside it.

- See all the shades of the rainbow coming into your aura and being absorbed by your body.

- Afterward, make sure you ground yourself and ask for protection from a black crystal, such as jet or obsidian.

You can absorb crystal energy by adding crystals to your bathwater and soak in their power!

HEALING MEDITATION

Holding a healing crystal in your hands while you meditate helps you absorb its powerful energy.

- Before you start, ask the crystal to work for the highest good.
- Hold your chosen crystal and place it by your heart, filling it with love and asking it to do what's best for you.
- As you exhale, let out all negative thoughts and feelings.
- As you breathe in, imagine the crystal's positive light move down your whole body.
- Picture this energy as a soothing, warm liquid radiating from your heart to fill you up.
- Sit peacefully feeling your crystal's energy making you whole and happy.
- Finish the meditation by thanking the crystal and taking several deep breaths to ground yourself.

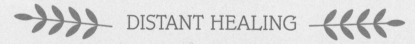 DISTANT HEALING

You can use crystals to send healing energy to people or animals, as well as areas of the world that need help.

- Hold a larger crystal in your hands.
- Focus on filling the crystal with intentions to heal whatever you've chosen to help.
- Say your wish out loud repeatedly into the crystal for it to absorb.
- Inhale deeply and imagine the light from the crystal filling you up. Exhale any darkness.

- Continuing to breathe in light until you are full of sparkling positive healing energy.
- Send this healing light to your chosen subject as you breathe out.
- Picture the healing taking place and the recipient shining with health.
- When you are finished, place the charged crystal on a photo of the absent friend, animal, or place to be healed, and leave it there for as long as you want it to work its magic.

Choose green or brown crystals, such as moss agate or jade, to heal the land or forests and animals. Blue gems, including aquamarine or blue coral, work wonders on the waters of the world. Tiger's eye or leopard-skin jasper help endangered species stay healthy and strong.

AMAZONITE

Amazonite is a blue-green or turquoise opaque stone, sometimes darker green with white lines.

Crystal care!

Cleanse amazonite by placing it in a bowl of water infused with mint to recharge its powers.

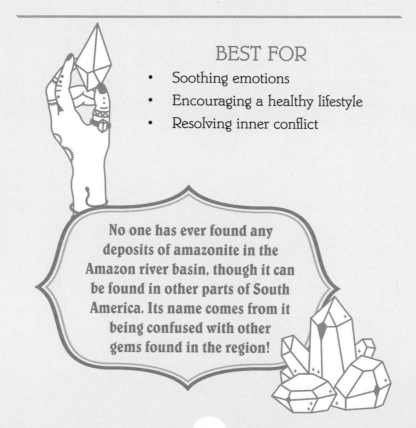

BEST FOR

- Soothing emotions
- Encouraging a healthy lifestyle
- Resolving inner conflict

No one has ever found any deposits of amazonite in the Amazon river basin, though it can be found in other parts of South America. Its name comes from it being confused with other gems found in the region!

WORKING WITH AMAZONITE

Create balance

Meditate with amazonite to get in touch with your inner wisdom. This will help you to understand what you need to do in the world … and how to put things into action.

Keep the peace

Often called the "Peacemaker Stone," amazonite enables you to see other people's viewpoints. When placed in a room, it will give out peaceful vibes for reconciliation and healing.

Help you speak

If you need to have a difficult conversation, put some amazonite in your pocket and let it help your words flow with compassion.

Three ways to use amazonite at home:

- Placed on your desk, amazonite will bring focus to your purpose and success to your work.
- A chunk of amazonite in the living space will encourage kindness in conversations.
- In the kitchen, it is said to encourage other family members to help with household jobs!

AQUAMARINE

Aquamarine is very light blue, clear to opaque. The name "Aquamarine" comes from the Latin *aqua* for "water" and *marina* for "of the sea." Aquamarine can have wonderful clarity, meaning that it dazzles with a bright, energetic sparkle.

Crystal care!

Cleanse aquamarine in a blue glass bowl of seawater or salted mineral water on the night of a full moon, rinsing with pure water afterward.

BEST FOR

* Increasing your inner wisdom
* Clearing communication
* Accepting your true self

This crystal-clear gem was once believed to be mermaids' treasure. Roman sailors sometimes carried it with them for safety at sea.

WORKING WITH AQUAMARINE

Soothe tired eyes

Place a small, smooth tumbled crystal on each of your eyelids for five minutes every night while you relax, and let its cooling, calming properties take effect.

Get rid of clutter

Having aquamarine in your home will help keep angry emotions away. It is also said to assist with getting rid of clutter—mental, emotional, and physical!

Send healing

Place a small piece of aquamarine on a photo of the person you want to help, and imagine aquamarine's healing energy filling their body, aligning their chakras, and bringing them back to full health.

Three ways to heal the oceans:

- Charge aquamarine with the intention to clean the oceans and protect all sea creatures.
- Place a piece of aquamarine on a picture of any endangered ocean life while seeing them thriving for years to come.
- Feel the sparkling health of the waters of the world in your heart, and let that energy ripple out around the planet.

BLUE KYANITE

Blue kyanite is made up of blue-white shards or blades. It is either opaque with a pearly sheen or transparent. It was named after the Greek word *kuanos*, meaning "blue."

Crystal care!

Kyanite does not absorb negative energy so it never needs to be cleansed, but you can boost its powers by leaving it near plants early in the morning.

BEST FOR

- Healing the animal kingdom
- Attuning yourself to the higher realms
- Increasing psychic abilities

Kyanite is also used in the automobile industry—for brake shoes, cutting disks, and grinding wheels!

WORKING WITH BLUE KYANITE

Send healing

Hold blue kyanite when you send healing energy to friends, family, and your pets. It will create a stronger link between you and the person (or creature) being healed.

Connect with others

In meditation, hold a shard up to your forehead (third eye chakra), and tune into a particular person that you care about. Try and sense how they are feeling and what they need to help them in any way. Then, think up a positive healing image in your mind, and send it to them.

Clear negativity

Blades of blue kyanite make excellent wands to brush away any negative energy from others, getting rid of anger and frustration.

Make a healing grid:

- Place rows of small kyanite shards coming out in six different directions from a central kyanite crystal.
- Sit by this grid and lower your gaze to focus only on the crystals.
- Allow your mind to wander, letting images and ideas take form as they arise.
- Meditate with this layout every night until you feel that the issue that was bothering you has been cleared.

CARNELIAN

Carnelian is a bright orange to red, semitranslucent glassy pebble, often containing lighter or darker spots and streaks.

BEST FOR

- Boosting healing
- Trusting yourself
- Improving your relationships

Ancient warriors wore this crystal around their necks to make them bold in battle, and it has long been believed to encourage bravery in shy people!

WORKING WITH CARNELIAN

Boost energy

Place a piece of carnelian on your stomach (solar plexus chakra) while lying down in meditation. Allow its surge of energy to work by balancing and grounding you.

Cleanse other crystals

If you have a bowl of gems in your home, add carnelian, which will cleanse them.

Three ways to help save the world:

- Gather with friends to use carnelian and send healing to ancient sacred sites to preserve them.
- Ask a carnelian crystal to heal the environment around it, then bury it in the earth.
- Make an essence of carnelian with water, and pour this on the ground, asking it to protect the world.

Hematite

Hematite is a metallic, silvery, heavy iron oxide, sometimes found in brown-red shades. It forms in rough rosettes but is more often found smoothed and shiny. Although mostly a metallic silvery black hue, some hematite has reddish-brown streaks and marks in red when rough cut and rubbed against another crystal.

BEST FOR

- Grounding and balancing
- Soothing headaches and backaches
- Deflecting negativity

Early humans created cave paintings using the red pigment from ground-up hematite.

WORKING WITH HEMATITE

Attract opportunities

Hematite has a magnetic pull, which can attract the right opportunities to make your dreams a reality. It can focus your mind when you need to deal with practical problems, and boost your willpower.

Deflect negativity

Hematite was used for divination and polished into mirrors to deflect negativity in ancient times. It is useful to have one nearby when you meditate to keep negative energies from entering your aura.

Combat jet lag

Be sure to carry hematite with you during and after flying, as its power is said to help with the effects of jet lag.

Healing ritual:

- Lie down on your front, and ask a friend to place a one piece of hematite at the top of your spine, one at the bottom, and one in the middle.
- Relax with your head to one side, and picture the power of the crystal swirling up your spine, from the bottom to the top.
- Imagine any pain melting away until your whole body shines with health.
- When you are done, thank the crystal for its help.

Moonstone

Moonstone can be translucent white, dusky pink, yellow, or sometimes blue. All hues display a pearly opalescence.

BEST FOR

- Helping plants grow
- Linking us to nature's cycles
- Calming emotions

Moonstone is said to lose its silvery sheen if the person using it holds too much anger inside them.

WORKING WITH MOONSTONE

Outside

Use moonstone to help your garden grow! Plant up herbs three days before the full moon—traditionally the peak growth time for plants—and bury a piece of moonstone with them to make them grow strong and healthy.

Sweet dreams

Moonstone in the bedroom generally encourages peaceful sleep. Place a small crystal under your pillow to get rid of anxiety and nightmares.

A healing gift

Do you want to send healing to someone who is going through a difficult time? Hold a small polished piece of moonstone close to your heart, filling it with loving energy, then give it to them as a gift.

Different times of the month to use moonstone:

- As the moon waxes (grows larger), moonstone will become more translucent. This is the time to use it for manifestation rituals.
- As the moon wanes (grows smaller), this gem will grow paler and emit more gentle energy. This is the time that it is best able to calm and soothe your emotions.

RHODOCHROSITE

Rhodochrosite is vivid raspberry pink, rose-red, and orange, with swirls and circular patterned banding. It is usually polished smooth.

BEST FOR

- Healing emotional wounds
- Attracting new love
- Healing the Earth

In a cave beneath the Andes, there is a large, heart-shaped rhodochrosite boulder. Legend says that it is the heart of Mother Earth, which beats once every 200 years.

WORKING WITH RHODOCHROSITE

Feel bliss

Hold this crystal over your heart chakra in meditation. Rhodochrosite's peaceful energy will fill your aura, heal your past, and show that you are deeply loved just as you are.

Heal the world

Use rhodochrosite to send loving, healing energy into Earth. Tune into the gem's power and ask: "How may I best serve the world?" Let your joyful ideas lead the way!

Forgive mistakes

Meditating with this crystal helps you understand and forgive your parents—or anyone else—for mistakes they have made in the past, creating a more loving relationship.

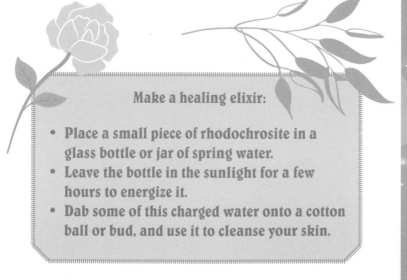

Make a healing elixir:

- Place a small piece of rhodochrosite in a glass bottle or jar of spring water.
- Leave the bottle in the sunlight for a few hours to energize it.
- Dab some of this charged water onto a cotton ball or bud, and use it to cleanse your skin.

The Best Crystals for Divination

How to Divine

Divination is the centuries-old practice of asking the spiritual world for help or advice. You can also use crystal balls, crystal pendulums, or a bag of smaller crystals to do this.

Divining dos and don'ts:

- Do cleanse your divination crystals before use.
- Do make sure you clear your mind of any worries or expectations before your start. You need to be able to fully focus on what your inner wisdom is telling you.
- Do take the time to formulate the question you want to ask. Keep it as simple and specific as possible.
- Do hold your crystals and connect with their energy, so that you can work together to get the best guidance.
- Do ask them to show you the truth of the matter as clearly as possible.
- Do keep an open mind about the answer—it might not be what it seems at first.
- Don't forget to note down whatever comes into your mind to look back at later.
- Don't make any hasty decisions. Take time to process any new realizations so that you can make the right decision moving forward.

QUARTZ AND CRYSTAL BALLS

Crystal balls have long been seen as tools of personal wisdom. Whatever gem they are made from, all crystal balls connect with the crown chakra and activate your psychic powers. This means that you can use them to tap into your inner wisdom and find answers to any questions about the past, present, and future.

Looking into the future using crystal balls was popular in fifteenth-century Europe, when people believed they could see spirits inside who would help them divine the future.

How to read a crystal ball:

- Light a candle, or use the light of the sun or moon to reflect into your crystal ball.
- Hold your crystal ball, and allow your energies to harmonize.
- Ask the question you would like answered.
- Sense any feelings, images, or words that come to mind.
- Place your ball down on a silk or velvet cloth.
- Gently soften your gaze and look at your crystal ball. It may appear to cloud over, but keep looking gently until any images appear inside the ball or in your mind. The different images may have significant meanings, or together they might make a story that serves as an answer.
- When you're finished, cover the ball with a cloth. Ground yourself in the present moment by taking a few deep breaths.
- Note down what you saw, thought, and felt, and anything you think it may represent.

AMETRINE

Ametrine is a sparkling transparent crystal that shimmers in shades of translucent purple and yellow. It is a combination of amethyst and citrine—and their names were combined to form the word "ametrine."

BEST FOR

- Concentration
- Healing
- Connecting you to higher realms

Ametrine comes from the Anahi mine in Bolivia. Legends say that the mine was given to a Spanish conquistador in the 1600s when he married an Ayoreo princess. It was lost for centuries and found again in the 1960s.

WORKING WITH AMETRINE

Help you meditate

If you find it hard to concentrate during meditation, hold a tumblestone of ametrine to clear stress from the mind, so that you can focus quickly and calmly.

Bring peace

Keeping a chunk of ametrine in the room when people are arguing can help end fights. The crystal encourages us all to accept other people's differences more easily.

Contact higher beings

Working with ametrine will enable you to contact higher beings, who can impart their wisdom to enrich your life. It can also protect you on journeys taken within your mind to higher realms.

Meditation ritual to visit other realms:

- Sit peacefully with a piece of ametrine in the light of a full moon.
- Imagine a door in your crystal that you can walk through into other dimensions.
- Picture it in detail, seeing its shape and texture.
- Go through that door into other realms—perhaps you will step into a fairy forest or to a past life!
- When you have finished exploring the realm, step back through the door, making sure to close it behind you.
- Take a few deep breaths to ground yourself back into the present moment.

EMERALD

Emerald is a bright green and sparklingly transparent beryl. This precious crystal has been treasured for thousands of years. The first known mines were in Egypt and date back possibly as far as 4,000 BCE.

BEST FOR

- Unconditional love
- Revealing the truth about relationships
- Boosting your psychic powers

This green crystal is connected to Venus, the planet and goddess of love. It is the traditional gift for anyone celebrating their 55th wedding anniversary.

WORKING WITH EMERALD

Stay safe

If you find that you are always listening to other people's problems, use emerald to protect you from being overwhelmed. The emerald's energy will also encourage compassion and forgiveness.

Open your heart

Wearing emerald during the daytime will open your heart, giving you the strength to make it through difficult times. But take it off at night, because this stone can make negative feelings rise to the surface.

Understand your truth

Meditate with emerald to clear your mind. You will find that you have come to understand the truth about what is right and wrong for you on a deeper level.

Discover past lives

Charge a piece of emerald with your intention to safely explore your past lives. Then hold it as you meditate, and explore any stories and emotions from the past that arise.

Heal your relationships

Wear this crystal as a necklace or brooch to activate the heart chakra. This can heal damaged friendships and restore broken trust.

IOLITE

Iolite is violet blue or indigo, and translucent, becoming yellow or smoky black depending on the angle it's looked at. Its name comes from the Greek word for "violet."

Crystal care!
Recharge iolite with natural light from the sun.

BEST FOR

- Boosting your psychic powers
- Creative inspiration
- Enhancing spells

Viking explorers used Iolite to help them find their way across the oceans. They looked through a thin piece to see the position of the sun, even on cloudy days.

WORKING WITH IOLITE

Get inspired

Sit peacefully, softly gazing at a piece of iolite and letting its appearance change as you move the crystal gently in your palms. Breathe deeply and allow unusual, otherworldly ideas and inspiration to come to you.

Focus and connect

Iolite helps you avoid distraction, so you can focus on what is most important in work and life. If you feel stuck while you are studying, it can encourage different ways of doing things.

Journey to higher realms:

- Lie down in a relaxed position holding a piece of iolite in your left hand.
- Hold a piece of onyx in your right hand for protection.
- Ask the iolite to re-energize your aura and align your chakras.
- Place the iolite on your forehead.
- Close your eyes, and let go of fear of the unknown.
- Iolite will help you move forward on your spiritual journey.
- At the end of your meditation, open your eyes and thank the stones.
- Don't forget to ground yourself back into the present moment with a few deep breaths.

LAPIS LAZULI

Lapis lazuli is deep, royal blue, flecked with gold iron pyrite pieces. Twinkling like the night sky, lapis lazuli is made up of a mixture of crystals including calcite, lazurite, sodalite, and pyrite.

BEST FOR

- Encouraging prophetic dreams
- Increasing psychic abilities
- Bringing peace and serenity

Many pharaohs of ancient Egypt, including Tutankhamun, built their tombs inlaid with lapis lazuli. If you are attracted to lapis lazuli, you may have had a past life in an ancient culture!

WORKING WITH LAPIS LAZULI

Improve your dreams

Lapis lazuli can boost your psychic powers if you place a piece on your forehead during meditation. Meditate with this crystal before bed, and your dreams will become rich with meaning.

Protect yourself

Wearing lapis lazuli anywhere on the body will relieve stress and bring a deep sense of peace and serenity. This crystal is a strong protective charm that calls on higher beings to keep you safe.

Headache cure

For help with headaches, simply hold a piece of lapis lazuli and sit quietly, imagining its healing blue light moving to the affected area. When you are finished, drink a glass of water to ground yourself. Make sure that you cleanse any negative energy from the stone afterward.

Onyx

Onyx is black with white banding or flecks like fingernails. Sources of onyx include India, Brazil, and Uruguay.

Crystal care!

Recharge onyx in sunlight to boost its powers.

Onyx is believed to hold memories! Pendants, rings, or earrings made from onyx will reveal the stories of its wearer to anyone sensitive holding them.

BEST FOR

- Grounding
- Protection
- Support

WORKING WITH ONYX

Prevent nightmares

Onyx gives you the strength to see you through the hardest times. Place a piece of onyx in your home to absorb sadness, prevent nightmares, and halt fear of the dark.

Heal past life injuries

Hold a piece of onyx, and it will guide you to a place on the body of a past life injury. When positioned there, it will absorb the stored memory of that trauma and send universal healing energy to help.

Support yourself

Meditating regularly with onyx encourages wise decision-making. It will support you through any life changes by guiding you toward the best path for you. It can also help you concentrate better!

RUBY

Ruby can be various reds from transparent light red and raspberry to the most valuable, deep red with a blue tinge.
The word "ruby" comes from *ruber*, which is Latin for "red."

Crystal care!

Revitalize your ruby by wiping it gently with a soft cloth, then leave it in the starlight overnight.

BEST FOR

- Increasing happiness
- Attracting romance
- Boosting energy

The Mongol emperor Kublai Khan was said to have offered a whole city in return for a large ruby. Rubies have always been associated with long-lasting love, and represent the 40th wedding anniversary.

WORKING WITH RUBY

Love life

Ruby brings passion and enthusiasm for life and love. It will increase your energy levels, motivate you, and fill you with a strong sense of leadership.

Dream better

Sleeping with a small piece of ruby under your pillow helps you understand what you see in your dreams—it will help uncover the meanings behind the images.

Star ruby

This is a variety of ruby with a six-pointed star naturally inside it. The ancients believed that star ruby contains three angels or spirits to help you learn about the past, present, and future. If you have a star ruby, try the following meditation:

- Sit in candlelight holding your star ruby.
- Look closely at the spot where the lines cross, and allow images to appear in your mind's eye.
- Sense intuitively what they mean to you, or write them down and research their symbolism.

Make Your Own Set of Divination Crystals

Create your own set of divination crystals by placing ten small tumblestones in a drawstring bag. Then, simply shut your eyes and draw out a crystal every morning to give you guidance for the day to come. You will need one crystal for each of these shades—orange, blue, purple, black, brown, yellow, red, green, white, and rainbow. Here are some suggestions:

ORANGE	amber, orange citrine
BLUE	aquamarine, lapis lazuli, blue lace agate, blue calcite, angelite, celestite
PURPLE	amethyst, azurite, purple fluorite, iolite, ametrine
BLACK	black tourmaline, jet, hematite, black obsidian
BROWN	tiger's eye, smoky quartz
YELLOW	yellow citrine, ametrine, yellow fluorite
RED	carnelian, ruby
GREEN	emerald, green aventurine, jade, green fluorite, amazonite
WHITE	clear quartz, moonstone
RAINBOW	labradorite, titanium rainbow quartz

Daily divination:

- Settle yourself somewhere comfortable.
- Ask your question out loud.
- Put your power hand (this is the hand you would catch a ball with!) in the bag, and choose three crystals, one at a time. Don't look in the bag, but choose according to which ones feel right.
- Place the crystals you've picked in front of you to discover their meanings.
- Hold each crystal that you've chosen, one by one, in your cupped hands. Close your eyes, and let images or words come to you for each crystal.
- Start your reading with these impressions, and then read the answer that each crystal gives from the list on the following page.

AMAZONITE Be a leader and stand up for what feels right.

AMBER Success is on the way. Take time to decide how you want to use it.

AMETHYST You're going through a big life change and may be feeling stressed.

AMETRINE Use your inner wisdom to sense the right time to step in to help others or yourself.

ANGELITE Are friends gossiping or causing problems? You may be called in to bring peace.

AQUAMARINE It's time to broaden your horizons.

AZURITE Your psychic and healing powers are getting stronger.

BLACK OBSIDIAN You have a lot of power at your disposal if you want to make a change.

BLACK TOURMALINE You should meditate on any confusing matters to help work out the best solution.

BLUE CALCITE Stay calm and keep the peace, even with those who annoy you.

BLUE LACE AGATE It's time to speak your truth on the matter. The outcome is likely to be positive.

CARNELIAN Believe in yourself and your talents. Set your own goals, and you will feel happy.

CELESTITE Don't worry about what may or may not happen. This keeps you from enjoying the moment.

CITRINE Your creative talents bring success. Make sure you tell people about your ideas.

CLEAR QUARTZ It's time to be optimistic. You have a great opportunity for new beginnings.

EMERALD You are successful and others don't like it, but stay strong—their jealousy will pass.

FLUORITE It's time to get in touch with your spiritual side.

GREEN AVENTURINE Speak up about what support you need to put your ideas into practice.

HEMATITE Make the most of the present moment, and new opportunities will appear.

IOLITE There's more than meets the eye about a new friend or situation.

JADE Compassion is needed for anyone who is being difficult to deal with.

JET You need to protect yourself from any negativity coming your way.

LABRADORITE Follow your heart to do what's right for you.

LAPIS LAZULI Now is the time to stick to your principles.

MOONSTONE Pay attention to your dreams, and listen closely to your inner wisdom.

RUBY Try to uncover the secret meanings in your dreams.

SMOKY QUARTZ Listen to your own voice, not other people's gossip.

TITANIUM RAINBOW QUARTZ The world is your oyster! It's time to get moving.

Index of Crystals

THE BEST CRYSTALS FOR HEALING

THE BEST CRYSTALS FOR DIVINATION

"The world is full of magic things, patiently waiting for our senses to grow sharper."

W.B. YEATS

Other titles in the series:
Astrology * Spells * Palm Reading